CW01021196

BARRYSCOURT LECTURES

BARRYSCOURT LECTURE SERIES

Barryscourt Castle is a fine 16th-century
tower-house at Carrigtwohill, Co Cork.
The Barryscourt Trust was established in
1987 with the aim of conserving,
enhancing and developing the heritage
potential of the castle.
    In 1996, the Barryscourt Trust
instituted a bi-annual series of lectures on
Medieval Ireland. These will deal with
aspects of medieval history, archaeology,
art and architecture, and will be
delivered by scholars specialising in the
period. The lectures will be published
individually and in compilation form.

Barryscourt Lectures IV
IRISH GARDENS AND GARDENING
BEFORE CROMWELL
Terence Reeves-Smyth

Published by the Barryscourt Trust
in association with Cork County Council
and Gandon Editions, Kinsale.

© The Barryscourt Trust and the author,
1999. All rights reserved.

ISBN 0946641 96X

Publication of this lecture
was sponsored by
Cork County Council.

Series Editor   Noel Jameson
Design   John O'Regan
                (© Gandon, 1999)
Production   Nicola Dearey, Gandon
Printing   Betaprint, Dublin
Distribution   Gandon, Kinsale

THE BARRYSCOURT TRUST
Barryscourt Castle
Carrigtwohill, Co Cork

IRISH GARDENS AND GARDENING
BEFORE CROMWELL

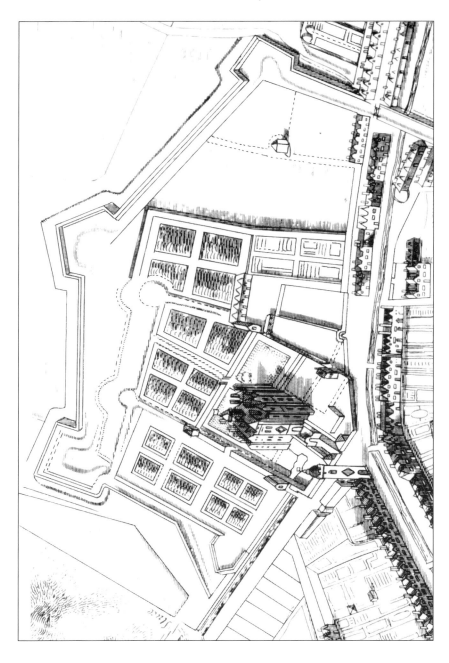

1 – Detail from a bird's-eye view of Belfast, dated 1685,
showing Sir Arthur Chichester's house at Belfast with surrounding gardens and courts

THE BARRYSCOURT LECTURES IV

Irish Gardens and Gardening before Cromwell

Terence Reeves-Smyth

THE BARRYSCOURT TRUST
IN ASSOCIATION WITH CORK COUNTY COUNCIL AND GANDON EDITIONS

2 – Tully Castle: view of the early 17th-century-style garden
created in the castle's bawn

INTRODUCTION

Considerable variation existed in the form and function of Irish gardens during the centuries prior to the 1600s, and although the range of plants was largely restricted to European varieties, gardens were far from colourless or uninteresting.[1] Culinary and medicinal plants predominated, but from medieval times, and perhaps even before, gardens were perceived not just in purely utilitarian terms, but also as places of leisure. Thus, physic gardens, orchards and even kitchen gardens were often designed for recreation as well as utility. The idea of the pleasure garden as an art form came fully to prominence in late Tudor and Jacobean Ireland, when plants were increasingly appreciated for their own sake and gardens were designed for ornament, amusement and as a means to indicate status or social achievement. Continental Renaissance ideas, exemplified in the use of terracing, statuary and other architectural features within coherent and symmetrical garden layouts, were well established by 1641 when Ireland was plunged into war. In the years that followed, there was little opportunity for gardening, and further developments ceased until after the Restoration of 1660.

Throughout their development from early times to the mid-17th century, Irish gardens were confined within enclosures. Like a picture in a frame, physical boundaries were considered an integral part of a garden's layout; walls, banks, hedges and fences were all employed, and these served to keep livestock and people out and to provide much needed shelter for the plants within. Garden enclosures were not unique to Ireland, but the frequently unsettled conditions of the country no doubt contributed to their prevalence; indeed, at times they also functioned as part of the defensive network relating to a manor or castle.

Enclosure boundaries are a feature of early gardens that may be expected to leave some sort of imprint in the archaeological record, while path layouts, flower beds, basins and other features can also leave traces in various forms. The value of analytical field survey and excavation in investigating such relict features has been fully demonstrated in recent decades, and garden archaeology is now an established discipline in Britain and elsewhere.[2] Undoubtedly, the most obvious and identifiable relict gardens date from the 1660 to 1740 era, when very structured, extensive and geometrical layouts predominated, but there are some good survivals from the pre-Cromwellian period. An example is the early 17th-century garden at Dunluce Castle, county Antrim, where flights of terraces and raised flower beds are preserved as upstanding earthworks in permanent pasture.[3] The quality of survival in this case owed much to the castle being deserted within decades of the garden's creation, although this is unusual as most of Ireland's great houses of this era either survived or were later rebuilt on or near the same site.[4] Consequently, the associated gardens were invariably altered or swept away by later activities – often a succession of garden layouts, each reflecting the changing fashions of its period. Such multi-period sites can be archaeologically rewarding in themselves, but ultimately our best source of information must derive from the minority of gardens abandoned at early stage.

In the long term, much of our knowledge of pre-17th-century gardens will inevitably derive from programmes of fieldwork and excavation, but to date the potential of garden archaeology in Ireland has yet to be fully realised.[5] Meanwhile, heavy reliance must be placed upon the historical record. Unfortunately, although documentary sources contain plenty of references to gardens and orchards, this by itself is of limited value beyond indicating that garden-making was widely practised in Ireland from earlier medieval times. More exact information on layout, content and size is scarce, due to a paucity of surviving records and to illiteracy among gardeners prior to the 1700s. Instructions were given verbally, garden catalogues were rarely compiled, plant acquisitions were often by exchange, and those purchased were seldom specified individually on bills. The difficulties are exacerbated by the backwardness of social history research in Irish medieval studies and by the fact that a great deal of manuscript material remains unpublished.[6] Nonetheless, much can be inferred from the available records, while comparative English material can be used in the generalities of the field.

3 – Aerial view of Dunluce castle gardens
showing terraces and raised beds

PREHISTORIC GARDENING

Horticulture is rarely if ever mentioned, let alone discussed, in the context of Irish or British prehistory, but the probability is high that some form of gardening existed at this time. Unfortunately, despite the wealth of evidence for cultivation from pollen studies, field systems and ard marks, we still know surprisingly little of the range and relative importance of the plants grown in prehistory.[7] Part of the problem derives from a lack of waterlogged deposits – the most valuable class of evidence – and our consequent dependence upon carbonised remains, supplemented by seed impressions on pottery. From these sources we know that naked and hulled barley, rye and primitive wheats, such as emmer and einkorn, were grown in the Irish Neolithic, but the range cultivated may have been more numerous than presently known as relatively few sites have been extensively sampled for charred remains. Furthermore, the food plants likely to be preserved in carbonised form are inherently biased towards those crops which needed to be parched over or in the domestic fire as part of the processing before consumption.[8] Most edible greens, notably root vegetables and brassicas, are unlikely to leave any identifiable trace, and although legumes (peas and beans) sometimes have to be kiln-dried or parched before storage, this may have been unnecessary in the Neolithic or Bronze Age if summer temperatures were appreciably higher than today.

It could be argued that many of the plants cultivated in continental Europe during prehistory were probably also grown in Ireland, provided the environmental conditions were favourable. Trade and cultural links extended over wide areas, and besides, it is unlikely that new colonisers would have abandoned their basic complement of seed stocks. As legumes accompanied cereals in the early advance of agriculture,[9] their early arrival in Ireland is likely.[10] The vine may likewise have had an early appearance, as grape pips, most probably *Vitis sylvestris*, have been discovered in early Neolithic levels as far north as Sweden, as well as in England.[11]

Alexanders (*Olusatrum*, *Petroselinum alexandrinum*), beet (*Beta*) and coriander (*Coriandrum*) go back to the Iron Age or earlier, and there is also continental evidence for use of the common goosefoot or fat hen (*Chenopodium album*) as a vegetable, and for the deliberate cultivation of other arable weeds, notably Pale Persicaria (*Polygonum lapathifolium*) and Gold of Pleasure (*Candina satina*).[12] Leeks, celery and carrots may also have been grown in Ireland during prehistory, but unfortunately, being so highly perishable, they will always be difficult to detect. However, the wild leek (*Allium babingtonii*), which grows today in the west of Ireland and is related to species found in south-west Europe, might be descended from such early imports.[13]

The value of plants to make and dye cloths was widely appreciated in prehistory. Flax (*Linum usitatissum*), which was harvested for its oil-rich seeds (linseed) and its bast fibres to make linen, was cultivated in Ireland from at least the early Bronze Age, and appears to have been widespread by early Christian times.[14] We have no direct evidence for dyes on Irish prehistoric levels as yet, but the sophistication of jewellery and personal ornaments in both the Bronze Age and Iron Age indicates a wealthy and fashion-conscious society which probably used clothing colours to denote the wearer's rank, as was done in early historic times.[15] In the English Iron Age, woad (*Isatis tinctoria*) was used as a blue and possibly pink dye,[16] while other dye plants known to have been cultivated from European prehistoric contexts include weld (*Reseda luteola*) and Aaron's rod (*Verbascum thapsus*) for yellow, field madder (*Sherardia arvensis*) for pink, and safflower (*Carthamus tinctoria*) for orange.[17] Such plants would probably have been grown in special gardens rather than alongside the arable.

———

4 – Woad (*Isatis tinctoria*)

THE EARLY CHRISTIAN PERIOD

It is clear that the Romans, during their four centuries of domination of Britain, were responsible for introducing a wide range of fruit, vegetables and flowers, as well as new methods of horticulture.[18] Some seeds and plants no doubt arrived in Ireland during the period of empire, but it was not until the 5th century, with the arrival of Christian missionaries, that any real semblance of Roman gardening techniques and plants were adopted here.[19] The church brought Ireland into direct contact with the Romanised world, introducing, among other things, literacy and a knowledge of continental lifestyles and values. In the monasteries, which multiplied in number during the 6th and 7th centuries, classical literature was avidly read, including texts on botany, agriculture and horticulture, notably Pliny's *Naturalis Historia* and the specialist works of the *De re Rustica*.[20] Horticultural expertise was undoubtedly also brought by some of the scholars who flocked from the continent to the Irish monastic schools and by monks returning from their European travels as missionaries or 'pilgrims of grace'. The gardening interest of some of these monks is illustrated by the story of Saint Fiachra, a Donegal nobleman, who travelled to France in the 7th century and founded a monastery deep in the forests of Breuil near Meaux. Here he created a garden so fine that he has since been regarded as the patron saint of gardeners.[21]

The early Irish monasteries took horticulture seriously in order to meet the demands of their self-sufficient lifestyles and to satisfy their communal or penitential dietary emphasis on vegetable rather than meat products. The size of their gardens has yet to be established, but they were almost certainly located within the termons or boundaries of the *monasteria*. Typically, these enclosures took the form of a curvilinear outer vallum or embankment, with an inner, eccentrically placed smaller one.[22] The church and graveyard occupied the inner precinct, while the outer zone would have contained the fenced gardens and orchards, with industrial activity areas near the perimeter, all interspersed with the monks' cells.

Modern excavation of these ecclesiastical enclosures in Ireland is very limited, but extensive work has been undertaken on a number of sites in south-west Scotland (Dalriada), where early Irish monasticism also flourished. At Whithorn in Galloway, one such *monasterium* produced clear botanical evidence for the cultivation of both medicinal and culinary herbs from the 6th century. Among the medicinal assemblages here, one contained elder (*Sambucus nigra*), hemlock (*Conium maculatum*) and woundwort (*Stachys arvensis*), while another included species with properties that were particularly appropriate to digestive problems, such as chickweed (*Stellaria media*), dog rose (*Rosa cania*), mustard (*Brassica nigra*), coriander (*Coriandrum sativum*) and dill (*Anethum grave lens*).[23]

While archaeological evidence remains sparse, the early written tracts are quite unambiguous about the existence of gardening both in the monasteries and among the population at large. These sources derive principally from the law-texts, annals, saints' lives, poetry and sagas, and mostly date from the 7th to the 9th centuries.[24] They make it clear that a prosperous farm often had an enclosed garden (**lubgort**) situated outside the **les**.[25] A whole range of garden plants are mentioned, and indication is given that their cultivation sometimes required specialist skills; for example, we are told that one of the seven officers of the church was a gardener (**lubgortóir**) and that on Iona, and presumably other monasteries, there was an officer whose duties was that of gardener (*hortulanus*).[26]

Vegetables, fruit and herbs were cultivated, and particular attention was apparently given to those with medicinal properties. The law tract 'Bretha Crólige', which seems to have formed part of the *Senchas Már*, states that 'no person on sick maintenance is entitled in Irish law to any condiment except garden herbs (**lus lubgort**) for it is for this purpose that gardens (**lubgort**) have been made.'[27] One plant often mentioned as a condiment for invalids, and apparently much cultivated, was leafy celery (**imus** / *Apium graveolens secalinum*), believed to prevent sickness 'and does not stir it up, prevents thirst and not infect wounds'.[28]

Identification of plant varieties from the early sources can cause confusion in some instances, but it is evident that the most frequently mentioned vegetable in the texts, **cainnenn**, was a bunching or shallot type of onion.[29] The leek (**borrlus**) was also commonly grown, possibly as a substitute for garlic, and can probably be identified with the variety *Allium babingtonii* found in western Ireland today.[30] Cabbage (**braisech**) featured in monastic diets, sorrel (**samhadh** / *Rumex acetosa*) was used in salads,[31] while skirrets (**cerrbacán** / *Sium sisarum*),[32] chives (**foltchép** / *Allium sechoenoprasum*) and kale (**meacain murrathaig**) were also cultivated, as were peas and beans. Other food plants not apparently mentioned, but likely to have been grown, include parsnip, beet, lettuce, radish and vervain, while in addition to dill and coriander mentioned above, monastic herb gardens probably also included such umbellifers as fennel, alexanders, parsley and lovage.

An important horticultural development of the period was the appearance of orchards (**aballgort**) containing apples, plums and possibly other fruit. Apples do not breed true from seed and most cannot be reproduced from suckers or cuttings, so in common with many other fruit trees, their cultivation demands the vegetative propagation of clones by grafting.[33] The technique appears to have had its origin in the far east, possibly western China, and to have arrived in the Mediterranean around 1000 BC or earlier.[34] The Romans, who employed a wide range of grafting methods, notably cleft grafting, root grafting and budding, are usually credited with introducing the art to northern Europe.[35] Earlier claims have been made on the basis of apple finds in prehistoric contexts, but these have proved to be the result of confusion between the small native European wild 'crab apple' (*Malus sylvestris*) and larger domesticated varieties.[36] As the evidence stands at present, it would appear that the technique of grafting, and with it cultivated apples, plums and possibly pears, were most likely carried to Ireland by the monks in the 5th or 6th centuries.

The early written sources make a clear distinction between native sour wild apples (**fiaduball**) and sweet cultivated apples (**ubla cumrae**). Indeed, one text apparently recognises the existence of different varieties of cultivated apples, and heavy fines were imposed for stealing them.[37] Many of the monasteries probably had orchards; at Tallaght, the Culdees were allowed to eat apples on festival days with their bread so long as 'each man's share of apples was three or four, if they be big ones; if they chanced to be small, each man's share was not to exceed the number of five or six.'[38] The garden plum (*Prunus domestica*), which like the apple was propagated by grafting, was also cultivated at the time (**áirne cumra**),[39] but neither the pear nor the damson seem to be mentioned in early texts, though they were widely grown in contemporary Europe.[40]

The much-quoted statement that Ireland had 'no lack of vines', written by the Venerable Bede (673-735) towards the end of his life, may not be such an exaggeration as some would believe.[41] Wine was indispensable for celebrating the sacrament, and the monks consequently needed a regular supply. Some importation was likely, particularly once the Norse towns were established in the 9th and 10th centuries, but transporting wine can be difficult and many monasteries were in remote locations. Considering the degree of self-sufficiency practised by the monasteries, and the probable mildness of the climate at the time, it is more than likely that the grapevine (*Vitis vinifera*) was often cultivated by the monks themselves.[42]

Some of the garden plants of the Early Christian period were grown for industrial purposes. Flax or **lin** (*Linium usitatissimum*) was widely cultivated,[43] particularly for linen tunics (**léine**), which were worn under the cloak.[44] Teasal (*Dipsacaceae sativus*) was possibly grown for fulling, and hemp (*Cannabis sativa*) for making rope fibre. The latter is an Asiatic plant, which was introduced to northern Europe by the Romans and was known to the Vikings.[45] Many dye stuffs are derived from plants, most notably woad (*Isatis tinctoria*), which is often mentioned in the early Irish sources (**glaisen**) and was clearly widely grown.[46] In one tale, the Queen of Tara is represented as having her own woad garden (**glaisengort**), while an 8th-century law-text gives details of some of the processes employed to obtain the blue dye.[47] There are also references to the cultivation of roid,

which Professor Kelly has convincingly shown was the dye-plant true madder (*Rubia tinctorum*), a native of south-west Asia.[48] The roots of madder
were used to obtain alizarin (Turkey red), and was widely available from
Roman times.[49] The onion (*Allium cepa*) was probably used for yellow dye,
as was possibly fairy flax (*Linum catharticum*) and dyer's rocket or weld
(*Reseda luteola*). Aside from cloths, a wide selection of dyes were needed
for the illuminated manuscripts, some of which were undoubtably of vegetable origin, though research has shown that many mineral-based dyes
were also imported for the purpose, such as red lead, verdigris, orpiment
and ox-gall.[50]

It seems likely that some garden plants were introduced with the
establishment of permanent Norse settlements from the 10th-century.
Excavations in Dublin and Waterford have produced considerable
archaeobotanical assemblages, bringing evidence of town diets and of
plants grown in and around urban areas.[51] Fruit and nuts were eaten, while
some of the herbs and vegetables found include leafy celery (*Apium graveolens*), carrot (*Daucus carota*), fennel (*Foeniculum vulgare*), radish
(*Raphanus raphanistrum*), mustard (*Brassica nigra*) and other members of
the brassica (cabbage) family. The evidence also suggests that fat hen
(*Chenopodium album*) and some members of the *Polygonum* genus (persicaria and knotweeds) were deliberately cultivated for food. Some of the
'weeds' found may have been grown for medicine, including chickweed,
mallow, hemlock, henbane and woundwort. As one might expect, the
assemblages are very similar to those found at York, though at York the
examination of vegetable tissue in addition to just the analysis of seeds
allowed such plants as leek (*Allium porrum*), woadwaxen (*Genista tinctoria*), Scandinavian clubmoss (*Diphasium complanatum*) and true madder to
be identified – plants which were probably also present in Dublin at this
time.[52] Most of these urban gardens, which appear to have been fairly rudi-
mentary, were located behind the street houses in small plots where they
jostled for space with sheds or byres and cesspits.

———

5 – Anemones
from Parkinson's *Paradisus*, 1629

THE MEDIEVAL PERIOD

Our knowledge of medieval gardens and gardening has been revolutionised in recent decades, thanks in large measure to the brilliant scholarship of the late John Harvey, whose classic work on the subject was published in 1981.[53] By piecing together a mosaic of information from many different sources, Harvey has enabled us to visualise gardens of the period in a way that had not been previously possible. He also established that medieval gardens shared similar characteristics across northern Europe, with a similar range of plants, so despite the fragmentary nature of the Irish evidence, we do have a very clear picture of the kind of gardens that the continental monasteries and the Norman settlers brought to Ireland in the 12th century.

Harvey and subsequent researchers have emphasised the central role of the monasteries in developing and disseminating horticultural expertise across Europe in the Middle Ages.[54] In Ireland, where the continental houses spread far beyond the limits of Norman expansion, their role was enormously important, and remained so until the Dissolution in the 16th century. With their emphasis on self-sufficiency and on a disciplined, corporate lifestyle, the monasteries practised a highly efficient system of agricultural, water and woodland management, and appreciated the importance of land drainage, soil enrichment, coppicing and crop rotation.[55] A knowledge of trees and plants was encouraged through well-stocked monastic libraries, often containing laboriously hand-copied herbals, and an exchange network of seeds and cuttings flourished among the monasteries, notably in the Cistercian order.[56] Herbs were grown for medicinal and culinary purposes, flowers for church decoration and religious festivals, and fruit and vegetables for guests and the community itself, which, at times, ate virtually no meat. For the medieval monks, gardening also had an important spiritual dimension: they believed that Adam and Eve's disobedience in the Garden of Eden – the Doctrine of the Fall of Humanity – meant that one avenue of seeking association with God was through gardening.

It is clear from the *Monastic Extents* of 1540 to 1541 and other documents that monastic gardening in Ireland tended to be focused within the area of the precincts.[57] These enclosures have been somewhat neglected in Irish archaeological research, though all the continental houses in Ireland adopted them, including the friaries.[58] The concept stemmed from the Rule of St Benedict, where clearly defined, self-contained precincts were advocated to ensure that the monks could be spared the temptation to roam abroad and encouraged to perform their necessary tasks within the spiritual sanctuary:

'The monastery should, if possible, be so arranged that all necessary things, such as water, mill, garden and various crafts, may be within the enclosure, so that monks may not be compelled to wander outside it, for that is not at all expedient for their souls.'[59]

A small minority of Irish precincts were delimited by walls, notably Kells (county Kilkenny) and Athassel (county Tipperary), but the majority were enclosed by earthen banks and ditches.[60] In their heyday, these enclosures, particularly those of the Benedictine and related establishments, were busy and crowded places, far removed from the quiet and tranquil places they are today. Some idea of their appearance can be gauged from the early 9th-century monastic plan of St Gall and from the 16th-century plan of St Vedast's Abbey, both depicting a whole series of gardens of all shapes, functions and sizes, jostling for space in the precincts amidst domestic and industrial buildings.[61] Analogous images are found in monastic accounts, for example, Norwich Cathedral Priory and Beaulieu Abbey in Hampshire.[62] In Ireland, the mid-14th-century Register of the Hospitaller's Priory at Kilmainham similarly shows a proliferation of vegetable gardens, herb gardens, pleasure gardens and orchards scattered within the outer and inner precincts.[63] These were wedged in amidst a motley array of structures, such as the brewhouse, dairies, forges, carpenters' shops, stables, granaries, barns, storage and food-processing buildings. There were kitchen gardens, hostiliars' gardens, obedientiary gardens and numerous garden

6 – Borage (*Borago officinalis*) in the medieval-style physic garden
created in the grounds of Grey Abbey, county Down

plots attached to the many *camerae* for permanent guests and others with-in the Kilmainham enclosure.[63] Many other monasteries also had infirmary gardens and some had almoners' gardens. All of these would have been enclosed in some way, either with paling or wattle fences and in some cases with stone walling.[65] Thorn hedges were probably not a feature of the precinct, but were commonly used to enclose manorial gardens of the peri-od, such as those on the Earl of Norfolk's Leinster estates.[66]

In some cases, the size of the monastic precinct was not big enough to accommodate all the gardens and orchards, and some had to be located outside.[67] Precinct areas mostly varied from one to twelve acres, though some of monastic enclosures in the Dublin suburbs, notably St Mary's Abbey, were much larger.[68] Areas under productive garden obviously var-ied according to the size and demands of each monastery, but it is worth noting that the great country houses of the 19th century, whose require-ments had much in common with medieval monasteries, needed between three and five acres of intensively managed kitchen gardens. The Cistercian abbey of Beaulieu had about ten acres of garden to support a community of 120 brethren and 250 hired workers,[69] so on this basis we could estimate that an abbey such as Graiguenamanagh, with fifty monks and sixty laybrothers, would have needed at least three acres of gardens and orchards – more than half the precinct area.[70] With the decline in the size of monastic communities in the 14th century, it is likely that garden acreages also fell.

As the location of the various precinct gardens was probably deter-mined by the layout of the monastic buildings, the kitchen gardens would be expected to lie close to the cook house. Practicality meant that grid-like plans were usually followed, as depicted in the St Gall plan, with raised beds, supported by boards or low wattle edgings, flanked by paths, which often doubled as irrigation channels. Most of the vegetables culti-vated in the monasteries, and by the population at large, were pottagers, so-called because they were cooked in a large metal pot to make pottage soup – the basic hot dish of the Middle Ages, which was usually eaten alongside the staples of bread and ale.[71] The main ingredients included leeks, onions, chibols, shallots, porrets, peas, broad beans, leafy beets and colewort leaves, flavoured with parsley, garlic and hyssop, and often including some meat or fish.[72] Many other herbs and seasonings were also grown for use in pottage or eaten raw as salad, but root vegetables did not come into general use until the late Middle Ages, when carrots, parsnips, skirrets, rapes and turnips were all commonly added to pottage.

A good idea of the range of vegetables and herbs available in Ireland during the Norman era can be obtained from a poem written in doggerel verse called the 'Feate of Gardening', dating to about 1300 and attributed to Master Jon Gardener. This treatise, which is the first coherent account of horticultural techniques in English, was probably composed in England rather than Ireland, but both surviving manuscripts have Irish origins and include references to 'all the herbs of Ireland'.[73] It contains sections on trees, grafting, viticulture, the onion family, coleworts, parsley and herbs generally, including a long list with seasonal advise and a concluding section on saffron. There are plants for medicinal and ornamental use, but the main basis of the list are potherbs, salads and sweet herbs, mainly for use in pottage or as flavouring. Some of these included alexanders, borage, cress, water cress, fennel, grounsel, lettuce, smallage, nepp (*Nepeta cataria*), orach (*Atriplex* and related genera of *Chenopodiaaceae*), radish, spinach and tansy. Principal sweet herbs and condiments include calamint, coriander, dill, dittander (*Lepidium*), hyssop, lavender, mints, sage, savory, thyme and wood sorrel. In all, one hundred herbs and vegetables are listed, excluding the probable varieties involved in many entries – a considerable number if compared with what was probably available in Ireland a few centuries earlier.[74]

A large number of the plants listed by Jon Gardener had medicinal properties, and many of these would have been grown in the monastery's infirmary garden, where they could be used by the resident *phisicus* or *medicus*.[75] Poisons such as mandrake, hemlock, henbane and opium poppy were normally included in the physic garden,[76] so a grid layout with raised beds was invariably used to ensure their segregation from plants which may have been used in cooking. Diet and health were, in fact, closely linked in medieval medicine, and fruit and vegetables were thus commonly included in the infirmary garden. Herbs and flowers such as lilies, roses, wormwood, polypody, dill, camomile, flag irises and saffron might be distilled or dried to make compound medicines, salves or tonics that could be used for general ailments, to treat blood letting or to protect against plague or disease.[77] These gardens also served as recreational areas for the convalescent monks, and often assumed an ornamental aspect with tunnel arbours, trellises and perhaps a small pond for growing aquatic plants such as waterlilies, which were used medically. Considering the important role some Irish monasteries played in caring for the sick, it is likely that a number of infirmary gardens covered large areas.[78] The one at Westminster Abbey occupied two acres,[79] so we should be careful not to assume that the physic garden was a tiny plot tucked away behind the infirmary.[80]

Physic gardens were often the location of beehives – a standard feature of monasteries and manors alike. Bees have been 'cultivated' in Ireland from pre-Christian times and have had a long association with gardening. They pollinated herbs and flowers, produced honey – used for sweetening, for mead and medication – and also beeswax for candles, writing tablets, seals and adhesives. Loghives appear to have been used by the Early Christian monks who were noted beekeepers, while wickerwork skeps were in general use by the Norman period; skeps of coiled straw seem not to have become widely employed in Ireland until the Tudor period.[81] There are references to 'bee-towers' or 'honey-towers' for keeping hives in medieval Ireland,[82] but it seems likely that most hives were kept in open-fronted shelters – a practice that continued until the early 19th century.

Beehives were sometimes located in the orchard, as were dovecotes, which are often mentioned in medieval accounts.[83] Most orchards were probably regularly laid out in a grid pattern,[84] and could be extensive in size; in 1303 the manor of Santry, county Dublin, had two hundred apple trees and one hundred pear trees, implying an area of at least three acres,[85] while the manor of Old Ross in Wexford was producing nine bushels of apples for sale in the 1280s.[86] Many of the monasteries could boast several orchards: at St Thomas's Abbey (Dublin) there were eight, Greatconnell (Kildare) had six, and Inistioge (Kilkenny) had five.[87] Some of these may have been 'cemetery orchards' – an age-old association that is depicted on the St Gall plan as rows of trees flanking the monks' graves.[88] Undoubtably, apples predominated in Irish orchards, most likely including varieties of Costards, Pearmains and Bitter-sweets, the latter being for cider.[89] The most widely appreciated pears of the period included Wardens, Sorells, Caleols and Gold Knopes, all of which were usually cooked and put into preserves, puddings and pies. Dessert pears may have been com-paratively rare, though there is one apparent reference to a *Bon Chrétien* in the prior's garden of St John's Priory, Kilkenny.[90] Plums and cherries were also grown, and other fruits might have included filberts, walnuts, medlars and perhaps even figs in some sheltered places.[91] The favourable climatic conditions that existed prior to the 14th century would certainly have suited figs, and, indeed, grave-vines,[92] for which there is some evidence in the form of both vineyards and winepresses, despite the fact that Ireland was known to be importing a great deal of wine from France during this period.[93]

Orchards were greatly valued in the Middle Ages for their blossom, and many were utilised as recreation grounds, complete with paths, flowers and arbours. Conversely, pleasure gardens often included flowering fruit trees as part of their design. Ornamental gardening was an important fea-ture of the period, particularly in the monasteries, where gardens were fre-quently created for prayer and mediation, known as 'paradises', or for entertainment purposes. Pleasure gardens also existed in the secular world, many, no doubt, being located within the bawn of the castle or manor. The Continental and English evidence demonstrates such gardens fol-lowed a fairly basic formula, being usually small, enclosed, square or rec-tangular plots with raised beds and much 'carpenter's work' in the form of trellises, fences and arbours. The area was often quartered with sanded or gravelled paths, leading to a central feature such as a pool or perhaps a bay tree (*Laurus nobilis*) – a symbol of constancy and a popular evergreen. Turfed seats, sometimes enriched with small flowers such as camomile and thyme, frequently edged the garden perimeter or occupied suitable corners, perhaps in association with potted plants, which were widely used in monasteries and elsewhere at this time.[94] Another striking characteristic was the large amount of woodwork employed in the form of garden furniture, fences, railings, trellises or tunnel arbours, the latter sometimes enclosing the area like a cloister.[95] These would have been wreathed with trained apple trees or climbers, such as vines or eglantine (*Rosa rubiginosa*), while the garden beds would have contained shrubs, flowers and herbs, the most popular being highly scented plants like roses and lilies.[96] Both white roses (*R.alba*) and red roses (*R.gallica* and *R.gallica* 'Officinalis') were grown in Ireland during this period, and, together with lilies and irises, were particularly in demand in the monasteries to decorate the church. Chaplets and garlands of roses were also regularly worn by the clergy on festival days until the Reformation. Indeed, the church often stipulated the payment of one or more roses, sometimes specified as red roses, as the annual rental for small holdings.[97]

Depending on their size, gardens of the period often included lawns. Invariably these were studded with flowers, such as sweet violets, periwinkles, primroses, daisies, cowslips and wild strawberries – the so-called 'flowery medes'. For Albertus Magnus, writing in 1260, 'nothing refreshes the sight so much as fine short grass', and it was for precisely this reason that the monastic cloister garths contained lawns. Indeed, except for a few very occasional references to roses, lilies, pines and junipers, all of which had symbolic values, there is no evidence for the growing of anything other than turf in the cloister.[98] The colour green was considered to have a tranquillising effect, as Hugh de Fouilly remarked:

'The green turf in the middle of the cloister refreshes encloistered eyes and their desire for study returns. It is truly the nature of the colour green that it nourishes the eyes and preserves their vision.'[99]

Isolated trees may have occasionally been planted in Irish monastic cloisters, though the famous yew at Muckross grows in the accumulation of debris which fills the court, and was therefore planted after the friars had departed.[100] There is some evidence for tree-planting in the medieval period, but the subject has yet to be fully explored and lies outside the scope of this paper. However, it must be said that the orthodox view that woodland planting did not take place until the 17th century is difficult to support in the light of our current understanding of underwood and timber management in Anglo-Norman Ireland.[101]

7 – Artichoke
(*Cynara scolymus*)

8 – Lismore Castle Gardens, county Waterford:
the raised walk above the upper terrace showing walls and corner tower

THE ELIZABETHAN AND EARLY STUART PERIOD

The gardens that evolved in Britain, France and the Low Countries during the 16th century remained fundamentally medieval in character. Features such as quartered enclosures, raised beds, tunnel arbours and trellises all continued, while the late-medieval vogue for knots or geometric patterns defined by perennial plants was developed into a major garden component, particularly in England.[102] From the time of the dissolution of the monasteries however, an undercurrent of change was slowly revolutionising garden design. The emergence of a new wealthy elite promoted the creation of larger and more magnificent gardens, while Italian Renaissance ideas, which flooded into Britain following the accession of James I, encouraged houses and gardens to be designed as single units.[103] In addition, exotic plants began arriving back in increasingly large quantities from newly discovered parts of the world, and gardening skills were improving, notably in the breeding of new flower strains with bigger double blooms. Above all, printed books started to make their mark on horticulture, such as Hill's *Proffitable Arte of Gardening* (1568), *The Gardeners Labyrinth* (1577) and Gerald's *The Herbal* (1595).[104] These and other publications made information on the form of gardens and their contents available to an increasingly wider audience, leading to greater standardisation in taste and design.

Ireland must have had many gardens during the Elizabethan and early Stuart periods; at least 3,500 are noted in the *Patent Rolls of James I*, despite the fact that only a small minority of the compilers considered them worthy of inclusion. Most were undoubtably plots for vegetables, but the great magnates had fine pleasure gardens and some of these were of considerable size. The tenth Earl of Ormonde's Tudor house at Carrick-on-Suir, built from 1565, had extensive courts on the north and west sides, no doubt filled with fashionable gardens, while the Desmond Roll of 1583 recorded that Newcastle West, county Limerick, had a garden with two fish ponds in the main enclosure and another three-acre garden and orchard outside the curtain walls.[105] Nearby, at Askeaton Castle, the Earls of Desmond also had a half-acre garden, 'triangular in plan, in which a fishpond lies to the south, all of which is enclosed with a stone wall'.[106] A bird's-eye view of Askeaton in *Pacata Hibernia* depicts this garden as being laid out in regular square plots, and while we have no further information, it is probable that each of these plots contained knots with delimiting wooden rails incorporating images of Geraldine heraldry.

The only visual representation of a garden during this period in Ireland is a bird's-eye view of the Master's garden at Trinity College, Dublin, in the 1590s. This depicts a large plot divided into compartments of different designs – a closed knot of diamonds and rectangles containing flowers, another with some form of emblematic design, one incorporating roses, and an open knot, presumably with coloured sands. There are no planting details, but in 1605 Harry Holland signed a deed allowing him 'the use and possession of the College's five gardens and the great orchard', being permitted to take half of 'all the herbs, lavender, roses and fruit of the trees'. He was required to grow turnips, cabbages. parsnips, carrots, artichokes, onions, leeks 'and other things as they shall need for 30 persons or 8 messes as the cook shall think good'.[107] Little mention is made of the garden flora, but a wide range was commonly available by this time, such as wallflowers, jasmine, lilac, syringa, species of iris and lily, hyacinth, tulip and double carnations. Edmund Spencer refers to many of these in his poetry, and no doubt grew them in his garden at Kilcolman, county Cork.[108] His contemporary and friend, Sir Walter Raleigh, introduced a number of his own plants, including the sweet-smelling yellow wallflower from the Azores and the Assane cherry from the Canaries, both of which he established first at Assane and later at Dromona. In his garden at Myrtle Grove in Youghal, Raleigh also grew the American tobacco plant, but is perhaps best remembered for his role in introducing the potato, which had such rapid and remarkable success in Ireland.[109]

Raleigh was a beneficiary of the land settlements resulting from the expansion of government control in Ireland at this time – a policy that brought waves of colonists, undertakers and administrators in ever-increasing numbers during the first four decades of the 17th century. It was land owners such as these, the so-called 'new English', who were the most eager to adopt the Italian Renaissance fashion for designing gardens in strict symmetrical relationship with the house, often with terraces, stairways, waterworks and sculpture. An early example was Sir Nicholas Malby's great garden from the 1580s, laid out in front of his new mansion at Roscommon Castle.[110] For Malby and other members of his class, gardens were a very visible means of proclaiming newly found status and wealth. Many of the 'old English' also saw themselves as upholders of civilised (i.e. anglicised) standards in Ireland and were willing to create gardens in the new style, but most appear to have done so with rather less ostentation than the new English. The more traditionally minded Gaelic landowners however, appear to have largely rejected Renaissance ideas, and while we know comparatively little of their gardening, it is likely many continued to create late-medieval style gardens until the 1640s.[111] As always there were exceptions, and much may have depended upon a family's wealth, geographical location and intermarriage with other socio-political groups.

The richest and most successful of the new settlers in Ireland during this period was Richard Boyle, the Great Earl of Cork, whose garden creations at Youghal and Lismore are documented in his diaries.[112] His house within the town walls of Youghal, 'The College', which lay beside Raleigh's

9 – Youghal, county Cork: view of Boyle's lower garden terrace looking towards the Sacred Heart Convent, formerly Richard Boyle's residence in the town

old home at Myrtle Grove, was flanked by two massive terraces, 160 yards long, cut into the hillside overlooking the town c.1612-14. The grounds occupied an area of about six acres, all typically enclosed behind stone walls with circular bastions. The terraces are depicted on a map of Youghal in *Pacata Hibernia*,[113] where they appear to be shown as a series of knot gardens, no doubt incorporating stairways, balustrading and statues, while some of the plants included a consignment of roses from Bristol in 1613.[114] The garden walls and terracing at Youghal are still present, as are those at Lismore Castle, which must count as the most impressive garden remains from this period in Ireland. The Lismore garden comprises a three-acre rectangular enclosure with enclosing high stone walls and turrets built in 1626, and contains a raised walk at one end and a series of terraces, stairways and a central path aligned on the town's medieval cathedral.[115] The planting details are unknown, but we can assume it contained topiary, globes, standard bays, pots of carnations and some statuary, all incorporated into elaborate knots, and perhaps even a fashionable *parterre de broderie* of clipped box which could be admired from the terraces above.

As at Lismore, pleasure gardens of the early Stuart period frequently functioned as part of the outer defences of the manor, often symmetrically flanking both the front forecourt, or bawn, and the house itself, thus allowing the gardens to be enjoyed from the main reception room win-

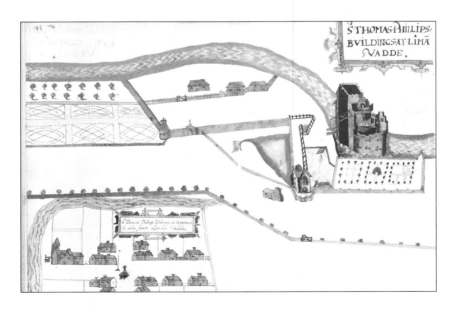

10 – Limavady
Raven's map for Sir Thomas Phillips, 1620

dows. Many of these enclosures had round turrets in the corners, which, in addition to their defensive role, probably served as viewing stations for the gardens. Indeed those at Galgorm, county Antrim (c.1620), and at Ballygalley Castle, county Antrim (c.1625),[116] were converted into summer houses during the 19th century. At Rathcline, county Longford, a network of rectangular towers protected the garden, and at Rosemount, county Down (c.1634), gun bastions were used.[117] There was also a bastion in the corner of Sir Thomas Phillip's pleasure garden at Limavady, as shown on Thomas Raven's 1622 drawing. Covering about a third of an acre to the north of the castle, this garden is depicted as having been subdivided into three large plots, each apparently delimited by topiary, with an arbour in the centre. The drawing also shows an enclosed kitchen garden and orchard located further away to the east, overlooked by a circular dovecote but outside the main castle defences.[118]

Some of the fortified gardens covered considerable areas. At Mallow Castle, the two gardens and orchard flanking the bawn covered four acres, and at Newtownards, the network of walled courts with flankers built by the Montgomery family in the 1630s occupied seven acres.[119] At Lemnagh, county Clare, the great house of the O'Briens, there were walled enclosures covering eleven acres, described in 1639 as comprising 'walled gardens, fish ponds, a pair of summer houses and a brick tower'.[120] Much still survives, notably an eight-acre enclosure which contains a brick-built summer house with classical niches, traces of fish ponds, a turret and a remarkable raised walk flanking the northern side of the enclosure. Walking was then a popular pastime and a number of gardens of the period were equipped with raised walks. Chichester House in College Green, Dublin, had a long, twenty-foot-wide terrace overlooking the gardens,[121] and at Jigginstown, county Kildare, there were impressive raised walks around a large rectangular garden fronting the south side of this palatial house built by Thomas Wentworth's from 1635.[122] As it was intended as a residence for both the Lord Deputy and the King, the garden undoubtably contained a suitably grand *parterre de broderie*, possibly with a central fountain. The raised walks here, from which the gardens could be admired, also had a defensive function, with their outside faces being lined with walling and brick-built turrets placed in the corners.

Earthen banks and palisades were also commonly used to protect gardens. Even William Bulkeley's fine house at Old Bawn near Dublin (c.1635), with its network of flanking courts, including a one-acre pleasure garden, was enclosed by a massive ditch.[123] A spectacular example of gardens being fortified with earthen banks was at Birr, where Sir Laurence Parsons enclosed about two acres north-east of the bawn in 1620-29. These gardens, defended with banks, bastions and a large stone-built 'garden tower', are depicted on a 1691 map of the town, and shown then to have contained three regimented rows of rectangular beds. Planting details are lacking, but each probably contained a knot or parterre.[124]

North of the gardens at Birr lay an extensive orchard enclosed by hedges. In the Birr papers there are records for the purchase of cherry trees from Croghan in 1622 and for cherry trees and plum trees from Thurles in 1625.[125] Orchards were now a very important component of Irish gardens, and the number of named varieties being planted was increasing rapidly. Many were being imported from England, but Ireland was already developing its own centres for fruit cultivation, notably in Kilkenny,[126] while the best published work on fruit for the period was written by an Irishman.[127] The Earl of Cork had apples, pears, peaches, nectarines, apricots and cherries at Lismore, and acquired Irish stock whenever possible; for example, Daniel Sullivan of Berehaven sent him Harvey apples and *Bon Chrétien* and Bergamotte pears, in addition to *arbutus* or cane apples for his garden

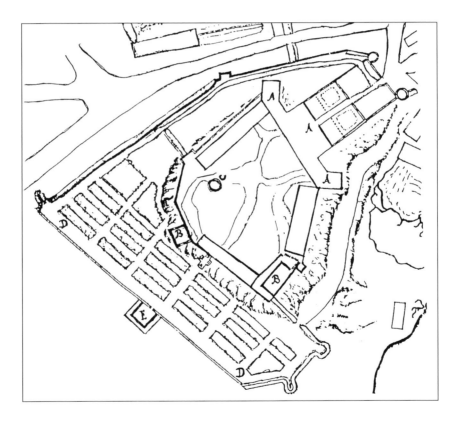

11 – Detail from Michael Richard's 'Plan of the town and castle at Birr' showing the castle bawn and gardens in 1691

in England.[128] Quinces, bullaces, mulberries, medlars, filberts and damsons were also available at this time, and the various fruit trees, either full or half standards, were normally planted in a quincunx,[129] often with an underplanting of grass enriched with sweet violets, spring bulbs, strawberries and perhaps the occasional rose bush. As in medieval times, the orchard was frequently treated as a pleasure ground, with straight paths, perhaps bordered with gooseberries or common berberis, aligned upon statuary, bowers or a summer house.

There were, of course, many palisaded or walled gardens of the period, which were not defensive in the military sense. At Dungiven, county Derry, the formal garden attached to the rear of Captain Doddington's gabled house and bawn was enclosed by a plain wall without turrets. The garden here, as depicted on Raven's 1622 plan, shows a quartered layout, with each of the four plots containing a diagonal arrangement of knots focused upon a central feature.[130] No doubt many other such houses had similar gardens; at Monea, county Fermanagh, for example, there is clear archaeological evidence for such an enclosure, presumably originally palisaded, flanking one side of the house and bawn. The gardens at Dunluce, county Antrim, which contained terraces, raised beds and a bowling green among its features, were also apparently enclosed on the landward side by a palisade.[131]

Whereas most gardens and orchards flanked the bawn or main fortified enclosure of Irish early 17th-century houses, some bawns were themselves large enough to accommodate gardens. Thomas Raven's plan of Macosquin, county Derry, shows the house in the centre of a large rectangular bawn, flanked by garden courts down one side,[132] while Sir Toby Caulfield's fine Renaissance house within the star-shaped fort of Charlemont, county Armagh (c.1622-24), was similarly surrounded by symmetrical courts, some of which almost certainly contained gardens.[133] A plan of the fort at Monaghan, built by Sir Edward Blaney in 1614, depicts a layout of six square compartments, each with complex knots, and three rectangular fishponds, all axially aligned on the rear of the house.[134] No doubt Blaney's main house at Castleblaney had a similarly grand garden, but the plan of this fort, like so many other surveys of the period, unfortunately did not include the gardens.[135]

Some of the smaller plantation bawns of this period might have contained gardens. At Tully, county Fermanagh, excavations in the 1970s revealed a series of cobbled paths, which were subsequently used as the base for a garden reconstruction.[136] However, most such bawns probably served as forecourts, and, as such, would have been treated in a manner typical of entrance courts in England throughout the 17th century. Normally this involved a wide path down the centre, a cross path and perimeter paths, the latter often running close to the walls. The square or rectangular areas created by this arrangement were occupied, not with knots or parterres, but with grass *plats*, and at the more pretentious houses these *plats* would have been delimited with topiary, with perhaps a statue or urn in the centre of each. Few, if any, flowers would have been included in what was a very masculine affair intended to project a sense of dignity to the house.[137] The front court at Portumna (c.1620), undoubtably the most dramatic bawn-court in Ireland,[138] was almost certainly treated in this way, as were, in all probability, other bawns of the period, such as Burntcourt (county Tipperary) and Coppinger's Court (county Cork).

The use of grass to make hand-cut designs in gardens, known as *Parterres à l'anglaise* or *gazon coupé*, was apparently starting to become popular at this time.[139] An amusing reference to something like this form of gardening comes from Sir William Brereton's visit to the Lord Primate of Ireland's palace in Drogheda in 1635, where he found a:

'pretty neat garden and over against the window in the gallery end, upon a bank, these words in fair letters are written: 'O MAN, REMEMBER THE LAST GREAT DAY. The bank is bare, the proportion of the letters is framed out in grass.'[140]

In the same year, Brereton also visited other houses and gardens, such as Lord Conway's manor at Lisburn, but it was Joymount in Carrickfergus and Belfast Castle which impressed him most. Both houses belonged to Sir Arthur Chichester, the Lord Deputy of Ireland from 1605 to 1616, and both reflected his considerable wealth, status and power.

Joymount, named in honour of Chichester's patron Lord Mountjoy, was built between 1610 and 1618. It is depicted on Phillip's map of Carrickfergus of 1685 (with inset view) as a fine three-storey 'stately house' with mullioned windows and projecting bays, approached from the south over a drawbridge and through a gatetower with domed corner turrets leading axially into a walled forecourt.[141] East of the house Brereton found:

'a graceful terrace and a walk before the house as at Denton, my Lord Fairfax's house. A fine garden and mightly spacious orchards and as they say have a goodly store of fruit. I observed on either side of this garden and twixt the garden and orchard a dove house placed one opposite the other, a most convenient place for apricockes.'[142]

From contemporary maps it can be established that this 'fine garden' was a rectangular half-acre plot bordering the east side of the house. It was divided by paths into four sections, with a circle, perhaps a basin and fountain, in the centre. A pair of dovecotes symmetrically flanked each side of this garden, with an orchard to the north and more gardens to the south. Just east of the garden and outside the town walls lay a large five-acre '*bordure d'arbre*', probably an orchard, crossed and recrossed by vistas of trees in a cruciform plan.[143] In 1683 Richard Dobbs noted that he had seen

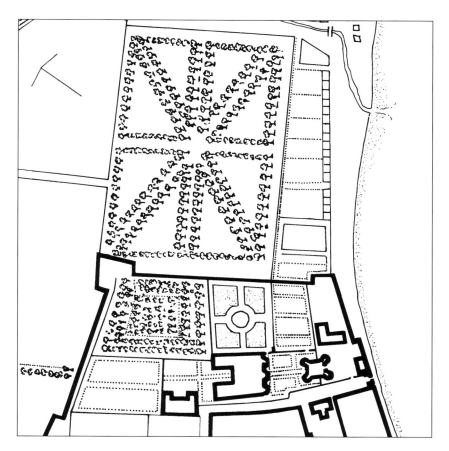

12 – A plan and inset view (c.1685) of Sir Arthur Chichester's house and gardens
at Joymount, Carrickfergus, built between 1610 and 1618

'cherries ripe (at Joymount) in May', and likewise had seen 'very good musk-melons here about 1658 and '59'.[144]

Brereton also admired Chichester's 'dainty stately house' at Belfast and his 'dainty orchards and gardens and walks planted out'. This was a tall, multi-gabled brick building begun about 1611, and, like Joymount, enjoyed the protection of the town defences – a factor which helped it to fully develop an extensive network of surrounding walled courts. These are depicted in a remarkable bird's-eye view of Belfast in 1685, where the house is shown to occupy the centre of a large walled court, flanked by walled gardens and orchards on the east, south and south west sides.[145] They contained among other things a 'cherry garden', an 'apple garden', a bowling green and arbours. There are also references to the growing of strawberries, currants and gooseberries, and to the payment of wages for rolling, cleaning, weeding and wheeling in ashes and cinders for the paths.[146] Further details are sadly lacking, but a garden of this quality would undoubtably have contained grass *plats*, knots and embroidered parterres, as well as statuary, topiary and waterworks – in short, all the trappings that epitomise Renaissance gardening in the period before the outbreak of war in 1641.

EPILOGUE

In October 1641 Lord Barrymore was hosting a dinner at Castle Lyons, his great house in county Cork, itself noted for its fine gardens and orchards, when it was announced to the disbelieving guests that rebellion had broken out in Ulster.[147] Within a year, those at the table, including the Great Earl of Cork and Lord Muskerry, would be fighting on different sides in what proved to be the most destructive and bloodiest war in Ireland's history. Over the next ten years, numerous great houses built across the country during the early Stuart period would be destroyed and their gardens abandoned, many of which would remain in ruins, never to be rebuilt. Ornamental gardening came to a halt, though vegetable gardens undoubtedly continued; the population still had to eat and gardens were probably a more reliable source of food than the more distantly located and less defendable fields of arable and livestock.

In the years following Cromwell's campaign, enough stability returned to the country for ornamental gardening to begin again. At Monkstown, county Dublin, the stern regicide, General Ludlow, laid out a fine garden 'famous for thy apples and thy pears, for turnips, carrots, lettuce, beans and peas'.[148] Also at this time, William Petty, who arrived in Ireland on leave from the University of Oxford, attempted in 1653 to set up a physic (botanic) garden in Dublin in co-operation with another army physician, Benjamin Worsley.[149] However, while new plants, especially fruit trees, began arriving into Ireland, it was not until the Restoration of 1660 that gardening was once again energetically embarked upon. In this new dawn, gardens were ultimately divested of their old enclosures and the symmetry of the house and garden was extended into the landscape through long perspectives. The concept of the 'designed landscape' had arrived, and with it a new age in garden history.

———

The author

Terence Reeves-Smyth is a Dublin-born archaeologist and architectural historian working in the Environment and Heritage Service (DOE, Northern Ireland). He has lectured widely and published books and articles on garden history, archaeology and architecture.

Acknowledgements

The author would like to thank the Barryscourt Trust for their invitation to contribute this piece on early garden history, and to Noel Jameson for his patience in awaiting its arrival. Thanks also to my colleagues in the Environment and Heritage Service for many long and productive discussions on this topic.

List of Illustrations

1   Detail from a bird's-eye view of Belfast, dated 1685, showing Sir Arthur Chichester's house at Belfast with surrounding gardens and courts (source: Map of Belfast, 1685 [NLI, Ms 3127-41])
2   Tully Castle: view of the early 17th-century-style garden created in the castle's bawn (source: Monuments & Buildings Record, Belfast [© HMSO - Dept of the Environment, NI])
3   Aerial view of Dunluce castle gardens showing terraces and raised beds (source: Monuments & Buildings Record, Belfast [© HMSO - Dept of the Environment, NI])
4   Woad (*Isatis tinctoria*) (source: Fuchs, *De Historia Stirpium*, 1542)
5   Anemones from Parkinson's *Paradisus*, 1629 (source: J Parkinson)
6   Borage (*Borago officinalis*) in the medieval-style physic garden created in the grounds of Grey Abbey, county Down (source: Monuments & Buildings Record, Belfast [© HMSO - Dept of the Environment, NI])
7   Artichoke (*Cynara scolymus*) (source: Besler, *Hortus Eystettensis*, 1613)
8   Lismore Castle Gardens, county Waterford: the raised walk above the upper terrace showing walls and corner tower (source: the author)
9   Youghal, county Cork: view of Boyle's lower garden terrace looking towards the Sacred Heart Convent, formerly the College of Our Lady of Youghal, Richard Boyles's residence in the town (source: the author)
10 Limavady: Raven's map for Sir Thomas Phillips, 1620 (source: PRONI, T/1576)
11 Detail from Michael Richard's 'Plan of the town and castle at Birr' showing the castle bawn and gardens in 1691 (source: T McErlean and B Jupp, Historic Landscape Survey of Birr Castle Demesne, 1996)
12 A plan and inset view (c.1685) of Sir Arthur Chichester's house and gardens at Joymount, Carrickfergus, built between 1610 and 1618 (source: Philip's town plan of c.1685 [BL: K Top 51-42 & 44])

———

Notes and References

[1] In historical perspective, gardening is understood to mean the culture of plants of any kind, while the term 'garden' denotes a plot where plants are grown. See J Harvey, *Mediaeval Gardens* (Batsford, London, 1981), pp1-2

[2] C Taylor, *The Archaeology of Gardens* (Shire Books, Risborough, 1988); AE Brown (ed.), *Garden Archaeology*, Council of British Archaeology Research Report No. 78 (London, 1991); D Jacques (ed.), *The Techniques and Uses of Garden Archaeology*, Jn. of Garden History, vol. 17, 1, special issue (1997). See also Royal Commission inventories and numerous papers in *Garden History*, the Journal of the Garden History Society

[3] No plan of the earthworks are published; see M Meek, *Dunluce Castle* (Environment and Heritage Service, Belfast, 1995)

[4] T Reeves-Smyth, 'The Natural History of Demesnes', in JW Foster and H Chesney (eds), *Nature in Ireland: A Scientific and Cultural History* (Lilliput, Dublin, 1997), pp549-72

[5] This is changing. In recent years many garden archaeological surveys (all unpublished) have been undertaken as part of the Great Gardens of Ireland Restoration Programme. In Northern Ireland progress has been made with the creation of a comprehensive Parks and Gardens Inventory and Register within the NI Monuments and Buildings Record (Environment and Heritage Service, Belfast). Garden excavations have taken place at Antrim Castle and Kylemore, but garden traces have incidentally been recognised on other excavated sites, viz. Barryscourt.

[6] The all too common failure to publish translations of manuscripts is also detrimental to research – most of us have better ways to occupy our time than grappling with Latin dictionaries.

[7] MA Monk, 'Evidence from Macroscopic Plant Remains for Crop Husbandry in Prehistoric and Early Historic Ireland: A Review', *Jn. of Ir. Archaeology*, iii (1985-6), pp31-6. K Jessen and H Helbaek, 'Cereals in Great Britain and Ireland in Prehistoric Times and Early Historic Times', *Biologiske Skrifter*, iii, 2, pp1-68; G Hillman, 'Crop Husbandry: Evidence from Macroscopic Remains' in I Simmons and M Tooley (eds), *The Environment in British Prehistory* (Duckworth, London, 1978), pp183-91; JM Renfrew, *Palaeoethnobotany: Prehistoric Food Plants of the Near East and Europe* (Methuen, London, 1973)

[8] A Fenton, 'Net-drying, pot drying and graddening: small scale drying and processing techniques', *Sage och sed*, yearbook of the Royal Gustav Adolfs Academy (1982), pp86-106

[9] D Zohery and M Hopf, *Domestication of Plants – The Old World* (Clarendon, Oxford, 1988; 2nd ed. 1993)

[10] No pulses have yet been found in Irish prehistoric contexts, Monk 'Macroscopic remains', p34. However, in England, the Celtic bean (*Vicia fabia celtica*) has been identified in late Neolithic levels, and the pea (*Pisum sativum*) has been recovered in Bronze Age contexts.

[11] G Jones and A Legge, 'The grape in the Neolithic of Britain', *Antiquity*, 61 (1987), pp452-55; G Rausing, 'The wheeled cauldrons and the wine', *Antiquity*, 71 (1997), pp994-99

[12] M Hanf, *The Arable Weeds of Europe with their Seedlings and Seeds* (BASF, Hadleigh, 1983); L Bouby, 'Two early finds of gold-of-pleasure (*Camelina sp.*) in middle Neolithic and Chalcolithic sites', *Antiquity*, 72 (1998), pp391-98

[13] WT Stearn, 'European species of allium and allied genera of Alliaceae: A synonymic enumeration' in *Ann. Musei Goulandris*, 4 (1978), pp83-198; EC Nelson, '*Allium babingtonii*' in WF Walsh and EC Nelson, *An Irish Florilegium II* (Thames and Hudson,

London, 1988), pp50-51

[14] Monk, 'Macroscopic remains' p34; V Hall, 'The historical and palynological evidence for flax cultivation in mid-Down', *Ulster Jn. of Archaeology*, 52 (1989), pp5-9

[15] M Dunlevy, *Dress in Ireland* (Batsford, London, 1989)

[16] JB Hurry, *The Woad Plant and its Dye*, ed. AR Horwood (Oxford, 1930); JH Betty, 'Cultivation of woad', *Textile History*, 9 (1978), pp112-17. Unlike many dyes, woad requires no mordant, but an alkali such as potash is necessary to make it soluble.

[17] F Brunello, *The Art of Dying in the History of Mankind* (Vicenza, 1973); H Godwin, *History of the British Flora* (Cambridge, 1975, 2nd ed.)

[18] Except for some excellent work at Pompeii, research into Roman horticulture is limited, particularly in relation to Britain. See S Applebaum, 'Roman Britain' in HPR Finberg (ed.), *The Agrarian History of England and Wales*, vol. i, ii (CUP, Cambridge, 1972); P Grimal, *Les Jardins Romains* (Paris, 1943; revised ed. 1969); E MacDougall and WF Jashemski (eds), *Ancient Roman Gardens* (Dumbarton Oaks, Washington, 1981).

[19] From the macrofossil evidence, we can be sure that the Romans in Britain had field bean (*Vicia faba*); leek (*Allium porrum*); pea (*Pisum sativum*); alexanders (*Smyrnium olusatrum*); coriander (*Coriandrum sativum*); dill (*Anethum graveolens*); fennel (*Foeniculum vulgare*); white mustard (*Sinapis alba*); parsley (*Papaver somniferum*); rue (*Ruta graveolens*) and savory (*Satureja sp.*). Fruits included sour cherry (*Prunus cerasus*); medlar (*Mespilus germanica*); black bulberry (*Morus nigra*) and plum (*Prunus domestica*). The cultivation of walnut (*Juglans regia*) is doubtful. The pernicious goutweed or ground elder, better known to Irish gardeners today as bishop's weed (*Aegopodium podagraria*), was introduced to Britain by the Romans as a vegetable, and probably also arrived in Ireland during Early Christian times. By 1380 it was known as 'the devil of the garden'; see JH Harvey, 'Botanical Incunabula', *Historic Gardens Review*, summer (1998), pp21-5.

[20] In chronological order, the four works of the *De re Rustica* are those of Cato (234-149 BC), *Varro* (116-27 BC), Columella (mid-1st century AD) and Palladius (writing AD c.380-95). Except for Cato, these authorities were widely read in monasteries throughout the Middle Ages.

[21] Originally just the patron saint of French gardeners, he also founded the monastery of Ullard in Kilkenny, and died in AD 670; see ES Rohde, *The Story of the Garden* (London, 1932), p60.

[22] K Hughes, *The Church in Early Irish Society* (Methuen, London, 1966); K Hughes and A Hamlin, *Celtic Monasticism: The Modern Traveller to the Early Irish Church* (Seabury, New York, 1981; 1997 ed. Four Courts Press, Dublin)

[23] P Hill, *Whithorn and St Ninian, The Excavation of a Monastic Town 1984-91* (Sutton, Stroud, 1997) with contribution from JP Huntley, pp252-95.

[24] F Kelly, *Early Irish Farming: A Study based mainly on the Law-texts of the 7th and 8th centuries AD* (Institute of Advanced Studies, Dublin, 1997); DA Binchy (ed.), *Corpus Iuris Hibernici*, 6 vols (Dublin, 1978)

[25] Kelly, *Early Irish Farming*, p368

[26] Kelly, *Early Irish Farming*, p250

[27] DA Binchy, 'Bretha Crólige', *Érui*, 12 (1938), pp1-77: 22-3

[28] DA Binchy, 'Sick maintenance in Irish law', *Érui*, 12(1938) pp78-134: 108; DA Binchy, 'Bretha Crólige', p36

[29] Kelly, *Early Irish Farming*, p251-53

[30] Stearn, 'European species of allium...', p83

[31] AT Lucas, 'Irish food before the potato', *Gwerin*, 2 (1960-2), pp8-43; AT Lucas, 'Nettles and charlock as famine food', *Breifne*, 1 (1959), pp137-46

[32] Professor Kelly gives the translation of the old Irish **Corrbacán** as skirret. However, some garden historians would argue that skirrets were not introduced until medieval times. Other than bulbs, the skirret is the first recorded root crop in England, being grown by the abbot of Westminster in 1273. It originally hailed from China. However, the water parsnip (*Sium latifolium*) is native to these islands.

[33] Cultivated fruit trees that usually demand grafting include apples, pears, plums and cherries. Those that can be cultivated without grafting include sycamore figs, olives, date palms, vines and pomegranates. The latter group appear much earlier in the European archaeological record.

[34] WC Cooper and H Chapot, 'Fruit production with special emphasis on fruit for processing', in S Nagi, PE Shur and MK Valdhuis, *Citrus Science and Technology*, vol. 2 (Aui, Westport, 1977), pp1-127; Zohery and Hopf, *Domestication of Plants*, pp129-62

[35] KD White, *Agricultural Implements of the Roman World* (Cambridge, 1967); KD White, *Roman Farming* (Cornell University, Ithaca, 1970)

[36] An apple recently discovered in a late Bronze Age context in Haughey's Fort, county Armagh, is due to be sent to Oxford for DNA testing (Dr Jim Mallery pers. comm.). It is most probably a native wild apple (usually 1.5-3.0 cm diameter), many of which have been found in European prehistoric contexts, such as the Swiss lake villages.

[37] Kelly, *Early Irish Farming*, pp259-62

[38] JGD Lamb, 'The apple in Ireland; its history and varieties', *Econ. Proc. of the Roy. Dublin Soc.*, 4 (1951), pp1-61; EJ Gwynn, 'The rule of Tallaght', *Harmarthena*, 42 (1927) 2nd supplement

[39] Kelly, *Early Irish Farming*, pp261-62

[40] Pliny noted twenty-two varieties of apples and thirty-six of pears. These numbers declined with the collapse of the Roman Empire, but it is clear from Charlemagne's list of plants that a considerable number of apple and pear varieties were being cultivated by AD 800; see R.von Fischer-Benzon, *Altdeutsche Gartenflora* (Leipzig, 1894); Harvey, *Mediaeval Gardens*, pp28-32

[41] B Colgrave and RAB Mynors (eds), *Bede's Ecclesiastical History of the English People* (Oxford, 1969; reprinted 1979), book 1, chapter 1

[42] There is a medieval reference to a vineyard on Iona; see J De Suse (ed.), *Ionae Vitae Sanctorum Columbani*, vol. 2, 25 (Leipzig, 1905), p292. It may be significant that realistic depictions of bunches of grapes are occasionally included on High Cross panels, as at Duleek and Old Kilcullen; see W Crawford, 'Carved panels representing the symbolic vine', *Jn. Roy. Soc. Antiq. Ir.*, 46 (1916), 181-2. The only reference to wine being imported into early monasteries comes from the Life of St Ciaran of Clonmacnoise, where a mention is made of wine arriving from Gaul coming up the Shannon, T O'Neill, *Merchants and Mariners* (Irish Academic Press, Dublin, 1987), p44.

[43] Monk, *Macroscopic remains*, p34

[44] Kelly, *Early Irish Farming*, p269

[45] H Godwin, 'The ancient cultivation of hemp', *Antiquity*, 41 (1967), pp42-9

[46] Kelly, *Early Irish Farming*, p264-67. Woad capsules have been found at the raised rath site at Deer Park Farms, county Antrim; E Allison, A Hall and H Kenward, 'Living conditions and resource exploitation at the Early Christian rath site at Deer Park Farms, Co. Antrim: evidence from plants and invertebrates', Technical Report 35, (Environmental Archaeology Unit, University of York, 1997).

[47] Kelly, *Early Irish Farming*, p265

[48] Kelly, *Early Irish Farming*, p267-269

[49] G Schaeffer, 'The cultivation of madder', *CIBA Review*, 39 (1941) 398-406. It should be noted that madder seeds have been found at Boho rath in Fermanagh and in association with E-ware pots at Tesshan crannog, county Antrim. Madder traces have also

been found at Deer Park Farms in county Antrim (Dr Chris Lynn pers. comm.). In medieval times, true madder was by far the most common dye for textiles, but there is no record of its import into these islands until the 14th century; see P Walton. 'Dyes on medieval textiles' in *Dyes on Historical and Archaeological Textiles*, 3 (1984), pp30-4.

[50] R Fuchs and D Oltrogge, 'Colour material and painting techniques in the Book of Kells' in F O'Mahony (ed.), *The Book of Kells: Proc. of a Conference at Trinity College Library* (Scolar Press, Dublin, 1994)

[51] GF Mitchell, 'Archaeology and Environment in Early Dublin, Medieval Dublin Excavations 1962-81', *Roy. Ir. Acad. Proc.*, series C, 1 (1987); S Geraghty, 'Viking Dublin: botanical evidence from Fishamble Street, Medieval Dublin excavations 1962-81', *Roy. Ir. Acad. Proc.*, series C, 2 (1996); B Collins, 'Plant remains' in C Walsh, *Archaeological Excavations at Patrick, Nicholas and Winetavern Streets, Dublin* (Brandon, Dublin, 1997), pp228-36; J Tierney and M Hannon, 'Plant remains' in M Hurley, O Scully and SWJ McCutcheon, *Late Viking Age and Medieval Waterford, Excavations 1986-1992* (Waterford Corporation, 1997), pp854-983

[52] AR Hall, HK Williams and JRA Greig, 'Environment and living conditions at two Anglo-Scandinavian sites', *The Archaeology of York: Past and Present*, 14 (CBA, London, 1983); AR Hall, PR Tomlinson, RA Hall and GW Taylor, 'Dyeplants from Viking York', *Antiquity*, 58 (1984), 58-60

[53] J Harvey, *Mediaeval Gardens* (Batsford, London, 1981);subsequent contributions include E MacDougall (ed.), *Mediaeval Gardens* (Dumbarton Oaks, Washington DC, 1986); S Landsberg, *The Medieval Garden* (Thames and Hudson, London, 1997); M Stokstad and J Stannard, *Gardens of the Middle Ages: An exhibition catalogue* (Spencer Museum of Art, Kansas, 1983)

[54] E and R Peplow, *In a Monastery Garden* (David and Charles, London, 1988); P Meyvaert, 'The medieval monastic garden' in EB MacDoughall (ed.), *Mediaeval Gardens*, pp23-53; T McLean, *Medieval English Gardens* (Collins, London, 1981; 2nd ed. 1994), pp13-58; CS Briggs, 'Garden Archaeology in Wales' in AE Brown (ed.), *Garden Archaeology*, pp138-40; G Coppack, *Abbeys and Priories* (Batsford, London, 1990), pp78-80

[55] Harvey, *Mediaeval Gardens*, pp57-58. Nurseries for grafts and seedlings were also established in monasteries across Europe; one existed at Kilmainham in the early 14th century: JC Walker, 'Essay on the rise and progress of gardening in Ireland', *Trans. Roy. Ir. Acad.*, 4(*Antiquities*, 1799), pp3-19; D'Alton, *The History of County Dublin* (Tower Books, Cork, 1987; facsimile of 1838 ed.), p313.

[56] The most comprehensive analysis of medieval Irish monasticism is R Stalley, *The Cistercian Monasteries of Ireland* (Yale University Press, London, 1987)

[57] NB White (ed.), *Extents of Irish Monastic Possessions 1540-1541* (Stationery Office, Dublin, 1943); see also, Irish Record Commission, *Irish Patent Rolls of James I* (Stationery Office, Dublin, 1966)

[58] See Stalley, *Cistercian Monasteries*, pp176-78, for a brief discussion of the precinct in an Irish context. Excavations in Ireland have been very focused upon limited areas, mostly within the claustral ranges. For a useful summary, see TB Barry, *The Archaeology of Medieval Ireland* (Methuen, London, 1987). Recently it has been accepted that the precinct needs to be the focus of future study; KD O'Conor, *The Archaeology of Medieval Rural Settlement in Ireland*, Discovery Programme monograph (Stationery Office, Dublin, 1998), pp142-44.

[59] J McCann (trans.), *The Rule of St. Benedict* (London, 1976), p74

[60] In some cases the medieval precinct incorporated Early Christian termon boundaries; see A Hamlin, 'A recently discovered enclosure at Inch Abbey, County Down', *Ulster Jn. of Arch.*, 40 (1977), pp85-8. Security became increasingly important by the 14th

century, and many of the walled precincts belong to this period. The largest and most impressive walled precinct in Ireland was St Mary's Abbey in Dublin (c.27 acres or 11ha).

[61] W Horn and E Born, *The Plan of St. Gall* (University of California Press, Berkeley, 1979); I Brou (ed.), *The Monastic Ordinale of St. Vedast's Abbey, Arras*, 2 vols (Henry Bradshaw Society 86, 1955)

[62] C Noble, 'Norwich Cathedral Priory Gardeners' Accounts, 1329-1530' in *Farming and Gardening in Late Medieval Norfolk*, (Norfolk Record Society, 1997), no. 61, pp1-92; SF Hockey (ed.), *The account book of Beaulieu Abbey* (Roy. Hist. Soc., Camden) 4th series, xvi; AB Bartlett, *Beaulieu Monks at Work; Production and Labour in the Account Book of Beaulieu Abbey, 1269-70* (London, 1979)

[63] C McNeill (ed.), *Registrum de Kilmainham: Register of Chapter Acts of the Hospital of Saint John of Jerusalem in Ireland, 1326-1339 under the Grand Prior, Sir Roger Outlaw* (Stationery Office, Dublin, 1932); C McNeill, 'The Hospitallers at Kilmainham and their guests', *Jn. Roy. Soc. Antiq. Ir.*, 54 (1924), pp15-64.

[64] Obedientiary gardens probably became more common in the later Middle Ages. Abbots and priors often had their own gardens, as at St Mary's and at Newgate (Hospital of John Baptist) in Dublin, *Pat. Rolls James I*, Pat. 8-2-lxvii, and *Monastic Extents*, p55. At Graiguenamanagh, the Abbot's garden was damaged by flooding in 1475; G Carville, *Norman Splendour: Duiske Abbey* (Belfast, 1979), p91

[65] For example, stone walls were noted at Armagh (Peter and Paul) priory, *Pat. Rolls James I*, Pat. 16-iii-530-vii; at Duleek some garden walls were plastered, E St John Brooks, 'Fourteenth century monastic estates in Meath', *Jn. Roy. Soc. Antiq. Ir.*, 83 (1952), pp140-49

[66] PH Hore, *A History of the Town and County of Wexford*, I (London, 1900), pp10-41; J Mills, 'Accounts of the Earl of Norfolk's Estates in Ireland 1279-1294', *Jn. Roy. Soc. Antiq. Ir.*, 22(1892), pp50-62. Garden boundaries at Old Ross, county Wexford, were sheltered by thorn hedging, palisades and ditching.

[67] As at Fermoy, county Cork, Hoggs, county Dublin, and Fethard, county Tipperary; see *Pat. Rolls James I*, Pat. 9 (4) xxviii; Pat. 13 (3) iii; Pat. 15 (3) viii. Urban monasteries often had garden plots scattered within and outside the town, as at Wexford; see *Pat. Rolls James I*, Pat. 4 (1) xxxii.

[68] Precinct areas are given in *Monastic Extents* and *Pat. Rolls James I*. It is important to recognise that these areas are mostly medieval acres or 'great measure' (gm), equivalent to about $2\frac{1}{2}$ statute acres. 'Small measure' is also occasionally employed; this is the same as the Irish Plantation acre of 1.6 statute acres. The English or statute acre was only occasionally used in Ireland until the 19th century; see J Mills, 'Notices on the Manor of St. Sepulchre, Dublin in the fourteenth century', *Jn. Roy. Soc. Antiq. Ir.*, 19 (1889), p35, n2.

[69] Beaulieu accounts of 1269, see Hockey (1975)

[70] A Gwynn and RN Hadcock, *Medieval Religious Houses* (Longman, London, 1970), p133

[71] JH Harvey, 'Vegetables in the Middle Ages', *Garden History*, 12 (1984), pp89-99

[72] Peas and beans from gardens were eaten green, those from the fields were used dry. Ireland was a major producer and exporter of field peas and broad beans in the Norman period.

[73] A Zettersten, 'The virtues of herbs in the Loscombe manuscript', *Acts Universitatis Lundensis*, sectio 1, 5 (1967), pp8-33; JH Harvey, 'The first English garden book: Mayster Jon Gardener's treatise and its background', *Garden History*, 13 (1985), pp83-101; EC Nelson, ' "This garden to adorne with all varieties": The garden plants of Ireland in the centuries before 1700', *Moorea*, 9 (1990), pp37-54.

[74] The following plants are included in Jon Gardener's lists: 'Adderstongue' (cuckoo-pint); agrimony; alexanders; avens; betony; 'bigold' (corn marigold); borage; brooklime; bugle; calamint; camomile; campion; caraway; centaury (lesser); clary; colewort; comfrey; coriander; cowslip; cress; water cresses; daffodil; bruisewort (daisy); dill; 'dittany' (dittander); horseheal (elecampane); felwort (gentian); fennel; feverfew; foxglove; garlic; glaswin (flag iris); gromwell; 'groudsel'; 'half wood' (?bittersweet); hartstongue; henbane; herb Robert; 'herb Walter'; hollyhock; 'honeysuckle' (?Meliotus); horehound (white); hyssop; langdebeef; lavender; leek; lettuce; lily; 'liverwort'; marsh (smallage); mints; motherwort (mugwort); mouse-war; nepp; Oculus Christii (wild clary); onion; orach; orpine; parsley; pellitory; peony; periwinkle; pimpernel; ribwort (plaintain); waybread (plantain); polypody; primrose; radish; 'red mayweed'; roses (red and white); rue; saffron; sage; St John's Wort; sanicle; savory (winter and summer); 'scabious'; senevy (mustard); southernwood; 'spearwort'; 'smearwort'; 'spinach'; stitchwort; strawberry; tansy; teasel (wild); thistle ('Wolf's'); thyme; tutsan; valerian; vervain; violet; wallwort; waterlily; woodruff; hindheal (wood sage); wood sorrel; wormwood; yarrow. See Harvey, *The first English garden book*, pp93-100. The absence of rosemary (introduced into Britain c.1340) helps to date the list; see JA Harvey, 'Medieval plantmanship in England: the culture of rosemary', *Garden History*, 1 (1972), pp14-21.

[75] Some monasteries had a series of separate infirmaries; Lexington in 1228 mentions some Cistercian houses having one for the monks, one for the laybrothers and another for the poor; Stalley, *Cistercian Monasteries*, p173.

[76] Dr Nelson has tentatively identified deadly nightshade (*Atropa belladonna*), and the opium poppy (*Papaver somniferus*) on decorated floral motifs at Corcomroe Abbey. Lily of the valley (*Convallaria majalis*) was also identified; Stalley, *Cistercian Monasteries*, p274, n40.

[77] NG Siraisi, *Medieval and Early Renaissance Medicine* (University of Chicago Press, Chicago, 1990)

[78] The 12th-century papal prohibitions against monastic involvement in lay medicine appears to have had little effect in Ireland, where some monasteries treated lay patients as well as their own brethren until the dissolution. Medieval lay medicine in Ireland tended to be a hereditary practice, at least in rural areas. For background on monk-physicians, see EA Hammond, 'Physicians in medieval English religious houses', *Bull. Hist. of Medicine*, 32 (1958), pp105-20; DA Amundsen, 'Medieval canon law on medical and surgical practice by the clergy', *Bull. Hist. of Medicine*, 52 (1978), pp23-43.

[79] JH Harvey, 'Westminster Abbey: The infirmarer's garden', *Garden History*, 20 (1992), pp97-115

[80] A monastic 'physic garden' has recently been recreated at Grey Abbey in county Down by the Environment and Heritage Service. It contains many plants that one might expect to find in such a garden, but in size must be regarded only as a miniature version of the real thing.

[81] Kelly, *Early Irish Farming*, p108-13; E Crane, *The Archaeology of Beekeeping* (London, 1983); E Crane, 'Bee bop a loo bole', *Arch. Ir.*, 6, no. 21 (1992), pp15-17

[82] There was a 40 ft. high bee-tower at Mellifont, and another at Clonmore, county Louth, 50 ft. high, built c.1230. The latter had a series of floors, each with louvred windows to allow bees to come and go. JK Watson, *Bee-keeping in Ireland: A History* (Glendale, Dublin, 1976).

[83] Some monasteries had several dovecotes or culvert houses. Mellifont had four within its precincts; *Pat. Rolls James I*, Pat. 3 (1) xvii. Most Irish medieval dovecotes were probably wooden structures with thatched roofs, but a handful of stone-built beehive-

type examples survive, notably Kilcooley and Shanagolden (both in county Tipperary) and Ballybeg (county Cork).

[84] Archaeology has the potential to verify this, as it has done at Dunstable Priory; see S Moorhouse, 'Ceramics in the medieval garden' in Brown (ed.), *Garden Archaeology*, p115.

[85] HS Sweetman (ed.), *Calender of Documents relating to Ireland 1302-1307* (London, 1887; reprinted 1974 by Kraus, Leichtenstein), p86, item 255

[86] Hore, *A History of the Town and County of Wexford*, p25

[87] *Monastic Extents*, pp2, 170, 185

[88] Landsberg, *The Medieval Garden*, pp36-8

[89] The various sorts of pippin didn't become popular until the 15th century. Cider may never have been the popular drink in Ireland that it was in England at this time, but cider presses are occasionally mentioned in Irish medieval documents; for example, there was one at Kilsaran Manor in Louth; see D MacIvor, 'The Knight's Templar's in County Louth', *Seanchas Ardmhacha*, 4 (1960-62), pp72-91.

[90] K Lamb and P Bowe, *A History of Gardening in Ireland* (National Botanic Gardens, Dublin, 1995), p12, n31 (from an early 19th-century source)

[91] Figs feature in Irish documents of the period, notably in kitchen accounts, viz. Kells Priory in 1382 and the Priory of the Holy Trinity, Dublin, in 1338; NB White (ed.), *Irish Monastic and Episcopal deeds AD 1200-1600* (Stationery Office, Dublin, 1936), p76; J Mills (ed.), *Account Rolls of the Priory of the Holy Trinity, Dublin, 1337-1346* (Dublin, 1891). Both figs and walnuts have been found in medieval archaeological contexts in Dublin; see Mitchell, *Archaeology and Environment*, p25.

[92] HH Lamb, *Climate: Present, Past and Future*, vol. 2 (Methuen, London, 1977), pp435-37; HH Lamb, *Climate, History and the Modern World* (Methuen, London, 1982)

[93] A vineyard is mentioned as part of the manor of Old Ross (see Hore, *A History of the Town and County of Wexford*), while in 1228 a winepress was noted by Lexington, probably at Jerpoint; Stalley, *Cistercian Monasteries*, pp45, 173. For a useful summary of the Irish wine trade, see O'Neill, *Merchants and Mariners*, pp44-57.

[94] Moorhouse, 'Ceramics in the medieval garden' in Brown (ed.), *Garden Archaeology*, pp102-6, figs. 9 (2, 3, 4). For turf-topped seats, see Landsberg, *The Medieval Garden*, pp51-3; Noble, *Farming and Gardening*, p10, n66

[95] This can hardly be understated, for most illustrations of medieval gardens depict wood-work, often a great deal, while documents speak the same story. Irish medieval gardens are unlikely to have been any different, especially as there was no shortage of either timber or joiners.

[96] For garden flowers of the period, see T McLean, *English Medieval Flowers* (Barrie & Jenkins, London, 1989); M Innes and C Perry, *Medieval Flowers* (Kyle Cathie, London, 1997)

[97] Usually to be paid on the feast of the Nativity of St John the Baptist (in June). For example, see E Curtis (ed.), *The Calender of Ormond Deeds (1172-1350)*, pp155, 163, 164, 186, 192, 225, 235, 237, 266, 277, 289, 298, 300, 301, 305, 313, 324, 339, 340, 345, 349, 356, 367, 382, 408, 450, 464, 588, 612, 629; Sweetman (ed.), *Calender of Documents relating to Ireland 1302-1307*, p81; White (ed.), *Irish Monastic and Episcopal Deeds AD 1200-1600*, pp75-6 (A57/99)

[98] Landsberg, *The Medieval Garden*, pp35-6; Noble, *Farming and Gardening*, p14, n96, 97, 98

[99] U Eco, *Art and Beauty in the Middle Ages* (Yale, London, 1986)

[100] H Leask, 'Muckross', *Jn. Cork Hist. Arch. Soc*, 45(1940), pp85-96. The yew here was probably planted in the late 17th century, when the friary was linked to the gardens at Muckross house by an avenue of elms. Young noted it had a diameter of two feet in

1776.

[101] H Jager, 'Land use in medieval Ireland: A review of the documentary evidence', *Ir. Econ. Soc. Hist.*, 10 (1983), pp51-65; A O'Sullivan, 'Woodmanship and the supply of underwood and timber to Anglo-Norman Dublin' in C Manning (ed.), *Dublin and Beyond the pale: Studies in Honour of Patrick Healy* (Wordwell, Dublin, 1998), pp59-68. Many of the monastic 'ash groves' or 'ash parks' mentioned in accounts could be plantations. Usually these were 'reserved for the repairs of the house'; see *Pat. Rolls James I*, Pat. 15 (3) iv. One of these groves lay within the precinct of St Mary's Dublin; *Pat. Rolls James I*, Pat. 8 (2) lxvi. See Pat. 3 (1) xxvii; Pat. 9 (4) xxvi; Pat. 10 (2) i; Pat. 17 (iii) lxxxii (Duleek).

[102] Knot-making first emerged during the 15th century and remained fashionable until the end of the 16th century. The spaces were either filled with coloured earth or gravels (open knots) or with flowers (closed knots). Designs were commonly adopted from textiles, tapestries or pattern books.

[103] R Strong, *The Renaissance Garden in England* (Thames and Hudson, London, 1979); J Antony, *The Renaissance Garden in Britain* (Shire, Princes Risborough, 1991). Both of these books concentrate upon the art historical and design aspects of gardens of this period, but without any good discussion of the plants used.

[104] D Mountain (Thomas Hill) *The Gardeners Labyrinth* (facsimile of 1577 ed., Garland, New York, 1982); J Gerard, *The Herball* (London, 1597; facsimile, Senate, London, 1998)

[105] TJ Westropp, 'The Desmond's castle at Newcastle Oconyll, Co. Limerick', *Jn. Roy. Soc. Antiq. Ir.*, 39 (1909), pp42-55, 350-68. It may be noted that Peyton's 1586 survey noted the 'great orchard' as four acres and the large garden as three acres. It lay on the west side of the bawn, occupying the site of the 18th-century walled garden.

[106] TJ Westropp, 'Notes on Askeaton, Co. Limerick', *Jn. Roy. Soc. Antiq. Ir.*, 34 (1904), pp111-32: 119; S O'Grady (ed.), *Pacata Hibernia*, vol. 1 (Downey, London, 1896), p63 (facing)

[107] EC Nelson, ' "Reserved for the Fellow", Four centuries of gardens at Trinity College, Dublin' in CH Holland (ed.), *Trinity College Dublin and the Idea of a University* (Dublin, 1991), pp185-222; see also Nelson, *The garden plants of Ireland*, p41; P Bowe, 'The Renaissance garden in Ireland', *Irish Arts Review*, 11 (1995), pp74-81

[108] Bowe, 'The Renaissance garden', p76; JP Collier (ed.), *The Poetical Works of Edmund Spencer* (London, 1891), p187

[109] JP Hennessy, *Sir Walter Raleigh in Ireland* (Kegan Paul, London, 1883); RH Salaman, *History and Social Influence of the Potato* (CUP, Cambridge, 1949; rev. ed. by JG Hawkes, 1985). The potato was recorded as growing at Grey Abbey, county Down, as early as 1606; see GH Hill (ed.), *The Montogomery Manuscripts 1603-1706* (Archer, Belfast, 1869)

[110] D Murphy, 'The castle of Roscommon', *Jn. Roy. Soc. Antiq. Ir.*, 21 (1890-91), pp546-86. The Essex estate papers have a drawing showing a grand avenue leading from the town to the castle. Avenues were perhaps unusual at the time, but apparently featured at a number of early Stuart gardens, as at Termon McGrath, county Donegal, Old Bawn, county Dublin, Loughmoe, county Tipperary, and Lemnagh, county Clare. The straight tree-lined avenue became a hallmark of demesne layouts in the late 17th and early 18th centuries; see T Reeves-Smyth, 'Demesnes' in FHA Aalen, K Whelan and M Stout (eds), *Atlas of the Irish Rural Landscape* (Cork University Press, 1997), pp197-205.

[111] Some idea of the plants grown by the Gaelic Irish during the early Stuart period may possibly be gauged from the lists of plants prepared by Philip O'Sullivan Beare, c.1620. It includes parsley, camomile, fennel, mint, tamarisk, hyssop, wormwood, rue, mustard,

rosemary, sage, cabbage, pumpkin, radish, lettuce, parsnip, sunflower and lily. Fruit listed included apples, pears, arbutus, walnut, chestnut, pine and mulberry; see TJ O'Donnell (ed.), *Selections from the Zoilomastix of Philip O'Sullivan Beare* (Stationery Office, Dublin, 1960) appendix A.

[112] AB Grosart (ed.), *The Lismore Papers*, 10 vols (London, 1868-8); D Townshend, *The Life and Letters of the Great Earl of Cork* (Duckworth, London, 1904)

[113] S O'Grady (ed.), *Pacata Hibernia*, vol. 1 (Downey, London, 1896), p27 (facing). This map dates to about 1620. For an earlier map of Youghal c.1580, see *Jn. Roy. Soc. Antiq. Ir.*, 19 (1868-69), p469.

[114] Grosart, i, p243. One hundred apples trees, prunes and quinces were imported from England in 1616 for the orchard, probably located outside the main garden walls to the south-west. In the 1640s, during the siege of Youghal, the garden leadwork was melted down for shot. The lower terrace is presently the convent garden, while the upper terrace is now a field, which fortunately has survived bungalow development because of its inaccessible location beneath the town walls.

[115] Grosart, iv, pp185, 206-219; Bowe, 'The Renaissance garden' pp75-8. The enclosure and adjacent orchards to the west are depicted on a map of Lismore c.1640; see M Girouard, 'Lismore Castle', *Country Life* (1964) August 6, 13. Defended garden enclosures were not unique to Ireland. There were good examples at Ware Park, Audley End and Hazelbury; see M Girouard, *Robert Smythson and the Elizabethan County House* (Yale, Lodnon, 1983,), p315, n28

[116] One of the turrets at Ballygalley (on the road side) is an Edwardian folly; the other surviving turret is original. It overlooks a raised terrace in the garden south of the bawn. For a useful outline history of Ballygalley Castle and Galgorm Castle, see CEB Brett, *Buildings of County Antrim* (Ulster Architectural Heritage Society, Belfast, 1996), pp23; 72-3.

[117] Rathcline plan, see NLI, Ms 8646 (6); W Harris, *The Ancient and Present State of County Down* (Dublin, 1744), p268

[118] Sir T Phillips, *The view of the Survey of the Plantation of the City and County of Londonderry* (PRONI, T.1576). Traces of the garden enclosures are still visible today.

[119] R Dunlop, 'An unpublished survey of the plantation of Munster in 1622', *Jn. Roy. Soc. Antiq. Ir.*, 54 (1924), pp128-45: 143; HG Leask 'Mallow Castle', *Jn Cork Hist. Arch. Soc.*, 49 (1944), pp19-24. During the 1640s a garrison was stationed in the gardens. The present house (built by Blore in 1837) stands within the old gardens, but the long terrace in front may be original to the early Stuart period. For Newtownards, see EM Jope (ed.), *An Archaeological Survey of County Down* (HMSO, Belfast, 1966), p260; Map of Newtownards 1720 (PRONI, T.2491/1).

[120] TJ Westropp, 'Excursions – Lemaneagh Castle', *Jn. Roy. Soc. Antiq. Ir*, 30 (1900), pp403-7.

[121] CP Curran, 'The architecture of the Bank of Ireland', *Bull. Ir. Georgian Soc.*, 20 (1977)

[122] HG Leask, 'New light on Jigginstown' in EM Jope (ed.), *Studies in Building History* (London, 1961), pp244-46; M Craig, 'New light on Jigginstown', *Ulster Jn. Arch*, 33 (1970), pp107-10. The house is 127 yards long with two front doors. Maurice Craig has suggested to the author that it may have been built to accommodate both the King and his Viceroy simultaneously in separate residences.

[123] HG Leask, 'House at Oldbawn, Co. Dublin', *Jn. Roy. Soc. Antiq. Ir.*, 43 (1913), pp314-25. Probably with an interanl bank or palisade. Unfortunately this site has now been demolished.

[124] 'Plan of the town and castle of Birr by Michael Richards, 1691' (Worcester College, Ms. YC 20 ccvi); T McErlean and B Jupp, *Historic Landscape Survey of Birr Castle Demesne*, vol. 1, report for the Earl of Rosse (Belfast, 1996), pp29-30

[125] The Birr papers have a payment (1625) for 'hedging 192 perches of the hedge of the orchard' and 'for rootinge the old apple trees and plum trees and throwinge downe of those bankes and raisinge the ground at the south corner of the orchard', the latter reference implying the existence of an orchard at Birr in the O'Carroll days. In 1643 the orchard featured in the Birr siege when Preston dug trenches across it. These trenches are still visible in the park; McErlean and Jupp, *Birr Castle Demesne*, p30.

[126] Fynes Moryson writing in 1598 described Kilkenny as memorable for its pleasant orchards, and says 'of the apple we have some fine old Irish varieties not excelled by any modern introduction'; F Moryson, *Itinerary* (London, 1617). Many well-known Irish varieties probably have their origin in the Tudor or early Stuart periods, such as the Scarlet Crofton, Irish Peach and Kerry Pippin. For a description of varieties, see Lamb, *The Apple in Ireland*, pp23-58.

[127] *The Fruiterers Secrets* (1604), later reissued as *The Husbandmans Fruitfull Orchard* (1608, 1609) by the mysterious Irishman, NF, of whom nothing else is known.

[128] Townsend, *The Great Earl of Cork*, p296. The strawberry tree (*Arbutus unedo*), Ireland's first horticultural export, was 'discovered' in Kerry and sent to England in the 1580s. It was much prized by gardeners during the 17th century for its scarlet fruits (uneatable) and white flowers; see Lamb and Bowe, *A History of Gardening in Ireland*, p15; EC Nelson and WF Walsh, *Trees of Ireland, Native and Naturalized* (Lilliput, Dublin, 1993), pp86-94. The Earl of Cork's house in England was Stalbridge Park, Dorset, long since demolished. The garden here was laid out by the famous designer Isaac de Caus; see Grosart, *Lismore Papers* (1886), p64; HM Colvin, 'The south front of Wilton House', *Arch. Jn.*, cxi (1954), pp181-90.

[129] The quincunx took two basic forms: the simplest had trees planted at the notional corners of a square, while the other more popular form had a fifth tree in the centre of the square, making a more complex pattern. Tree-spacing varied from fifteen to twenty-five feet.

[130] Sir T Phillips, *The view of the Survey of the Plantation of the City and County of Londonderry* (PRONI, T.1576). A substantial portion of Dungiven bawn has been excavated, see NF Brannon and BS Blades, 'Dungiven bawn re-edified', *Ulster Arch. Jn.*, 43 (1980), pp91-6; N Brannon, 'Archaeological excavations at Dungiven priory and bawn', *Benbradagh*, 15(1985), pp15-18. A small trench was put into the garden site during the 1982 excavations, but nothing was recovered. Sadly, the area was subsequently planted with trees, so the potential for good garden archaeology here is very limited (N Brannon pers. comm.).

[131] Earthworks are visible on aerial photographs in the Monuments and Buildings Record (EHS, Hill Street, Belfast)

[132] Proposed 'plot' for the Merchant Taylor's house and bawn. Probably not completed in form depicted on this plan; TW Moody, *The Londonderry Plantation 1609-41* (Belfast, 1939), p261, fig. 2

[133] Bird's-eye view of Charlemont c.1630 (British Library, Add. Ms. 24200, f.39)

[134] These fish ponds were for holding fish rather than breeding them. Similar ponds were a feature of other gardens of the period and may have been more common than we can appreciate on the basis of the present evidence. Examples included Old Bawn, county Dublin, Loughmoe Castle, county Tipperary, and Lemnagh, county Clare. The fish ponds within the walled enclosures at Newtownards, county Down, and Dalway's Bawn, county Antrim, may also be early 17th century. Fish ponds may also have been a regular features of medieval monastic precincts, examples being known at Cork Friary (*Pat. Rolls James I*, Pat. 13 (1) xxxviii) and Fethard, county Tipperary (*Pat. Rolls James I*, Pat. 14 (3) iii). For an assessment of fish ponds, see CK Currie, 'Fishponds as garden features, c.1550-1750', *Garden History*, 18 (1990), pp22-46; CK Currie,

Medieval Fish, Fisheries and Fishponds (BAR, Oxford, 1988), series 182.

[135] Monaghan and Castleblaney (Baile Loergan), plans c.1614 (TCD, Ms. 1209-32)

[136] M Meek, Tully Castle Guide Card (DOE (NI), Belfast, 1984). The garden work, created with plants known from this period, was supervised by Philip Wood of Enniskillen on behalf of the Environment and Heritage Service.

[137] It is relevant to note that such forecourts served as an outdoor extension to the hall, traditionally a male preserve, where tenants and others would be received by the master of the house. The earliest Irish depiction of such a court is a print c.1670 of Ballintober, county Cork, see R Ffolliott, *The Pooles of Mayfield and other Irish Families* (Hodges Figgis, Dublin, 1958), p150

[138] The present garden 'restoration' in the front court of Portumna Castle owes more to a vivid imagination than to historical or archaeological accuracy. The orchards and gardens at Portumna in the 1630s flanked the east and south sides of the house and bawn, while the west side overlooked the deer park, as at Mallow. No detailed study of the Portumna layout has been published, but for some background on the house, see M Craig, 'Portumna Castle, Co. Galway' in *The Country Seat: Studies in the History of the British Country House* (London, 1970), pp36-41; M Craig, 'Portumna Castle', *Gatherum*, 7 (1976), pp1-8.

[139] The *gazon coupé* was especially associated with gardens of the late 17th and early 18th centuries.

[140] W Brereton, *Travels in Holland, the United Provinces, England, Scotland and Ireland, 1634-1635* (Chetham Society, Manchester, 1844), p127; Walker, 'The rise and progress of gardening in Ireland', pp3-18. From 1625 to 1656, the post of Primate was held by Archbishop James Usher, so presumably he was responsible for this 'pretty neat garden'. The use of the term 'framed' might imply that the letters, which one might suppose were cut out of the grass, were all enclosed by a large surround of topiary.

[141] Phillip's town plan (NLI, Ms 3137-42)

[142] Brereton, *Travels*, p127-8. The reference is to Thomas, first Baron Fairfax (1560-1640) of Denton and Nunappleton, North Yorks.

[143] Town plans c.1685 (BL, K Top 51-46; 51-44; 51-45); Goubet's town plan of 1690-95 (NLI, Ms 2742-4)

[144] PRONI T.707/1; J Irvine, 'Richard Dobbs – notes from his description of County Antrim in 1683', *Glynns*, 7 (1979), pp35-49

[145] Map of Belfast 1685 (NLI, Ms 3137-41); reprinted by the Linen Hall Library

[146] Great Roll of Belfast 1666, see Belfast G Benn, *A History of the Town of Belfast from earliest Times to the Close of the Eighteenth Century* (Ward, Belfast, 1877), p242

[147] Townsend, *The Great Earl of Cork*, p196

[148] GT Stokes, 'The antiquities from Kingstown to Dublin', *Jn. Roy. Soc. Antiq. Ir.*, 23 (1893), pp343-56

[148] KT Hoppen, 'Sir William Petty: polymath 1623-1687', *History Today*, 15 (1965), pp126-34; Nelson, 'The garden plants of Ireland', p44

THE BARRYSCOURT LECTURES

The Barryscourt Trust
presents a series of bi-annual lectures on Medieval Ireland
at Barryscourt Castle, Carrigtwohill, Co Cork

I

BARRYSCOURT CASTLE AND THE IRISH TOWER-HOUSE
Tadhg O'Keeffe
October 1996 (published: May 1997)   ISBN 0946641 82X

II

THE IMPACT OF THE ANGLO-NORMANS ON MUNSTER
AF O'Brien
May 1997 (published: October 1997)   ISBN 0946641 838

III

TECHNOLOGICAL CHANGE IN ANGLO-NORMAN MUNSTER
Colin Rynne
October 1997 (published: April 1998)   ISBN 0946641 846

IV

IRISH GARDENS AND GARDENING BEFORE CROMWELL
Terence Reeves-Smyth
May 1998 (for publication: February 1999)   ISBN 0946641 96X

V

OUTSIDE THE TOWER – RECENT EXCAVATIONS AT BARRYSCOURT
Dave Pollock
October 1998 (for publication: March 1999)   ISBN 0946641 978

VI

BARRYSCOURT CASTLE REFURBISHED
Victor Chinnery
May 1999 (for publication: July 1999)   ISBN 0946846 197

VII

LANDSCAPE AND SETTLEMENT IN EAST CORK, 1100-1700
Kieran O'Conor
October 1999 (for publication: December 1999)   ISBN 0946846 197

For further details on the lecture series, contact:
The Barryscourt Trust, Barryscourt Castle, Carrigtwohill, Co Cork (tel 021-883864).

The Barryscourt lectures will be published individually,
and a clothbound compilation will be published at three-yearly intervals.
For further details on the publications, or to order copies, contact: Gandon Distribution
Oysterhaven, Kinsale, Co Cork (tel 021-770830 / fax 021-770755).